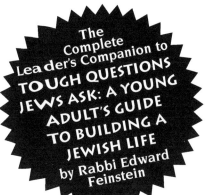

The Complete Leader's Companion to TOUGH QUESTIONS JEWS ASK: A YOUNG ADULT'S GUIDE TO BUILDING A JEWISH LIFE by Rabbi Edward Feinstein

TOUGH QUESTIONS JEWS ASK

TEACHER'S GUIDE

Rabbi Edward Feinstein

JEWISH LIGHTS Publishing

Tough Questions Jews Ask Teacher's Guide

© 2004 by Edward Feinstein

ISBN 978-1-58023-187-9 (pbk.)
ISBN 978-1-68336-470-2 (hc)

Manufactured in the United States of America

Published by Jewish Lights Publishing
www.jewishlights.com

Contents

Introduction

Four kinds of Jews sit before us at the Seder table: the wise, the wicked, the simple, and the one who cannot ask. The same four sit before us in class: the engaged, the alienated, the indifferent, and the silent. It's the last, the silent one, who is the most difficult and the most important. Why has he no questions? Is her silence an inability to speak up, to join the conversation, or does it reflect something deeper? Perhaps he is silent because he has come to believe that we have no answers to his questions. Perhaps she is silent because each time she asked, her questions were dismissed, shunted aside, hushed up, and now she has given up on us, given up on our ability to answer her deepest, most troubling questions.

Tough Questions Jews Ask was written for all our children, but most especially for the silent child. It was written to renew our connection with this child, to bring him or her into a conversation about the deepest questions of human life, and to demonstrate that Jewish faith and tradition has something important to say in response to these questions.

The aim of this teacher's guide is to assist you in organizing a course around this book. We envision a series of conversations, thirty minutes to an hour long, about the tough questions of being human and some Jewish responses to those questions. For each conversation, we will provide the:

OPENING: For an "induction set" or "opening hook," *Tough Questions Jews Ask* presents the experience of a classroom of kids in dialogue with their rabbi. You may find that your students, like the kids in the book, already have serious questions and are ready to jump into the conversation. Be sure to complement kids on their questions. If a question asked isn't the one you're ready to use this week, write it down and hold it somewhere to be presented in a later session. You might keep a "Questions Box" in your classroom or a list on your blackboard. In case your students need a bit of inspiration and guidance, we provide an opening for each conversation that sets out the question and a way to make the conversation engaging.

QUESTIONS FOR DISCUSSION: Sometimes discussions of tough questions need strong guidance and direction. Sometimes there is value in just letting discussions flow. You decide. To guide and further stimulate these discussions, we present excerpts from

Tough Questions followed by a series of discussion questions. It is important that students understand that discussions of tough questions are not just abstract, academic exercises. Our beliefs matter. They bear consequences in how we live. They determine the way we feel about ourselves and our world. They help us choose what's important to us. Our discussion questions help students understand what's at stake in these conversations.

SOURCES: The Jewish religious tradition is itself a conversation about life's important questions. Judaism is a tradition of many voices. Over the centuries, these questions have been discussed and argued over countless times. For each question there are multiple answers found among the sources of the tradition's texts. We want students to hear some of the voices of the Jewish tradition as they debate these important issues. We present a selection from these texts for each conversation, as well as references to others you might explore. After each text selection, you'll find some helpful commentary designed to invite students to join the tradition's conversation.

At the close of each conversation, present some questions that will help students solidify their opinions into coherent beliefs. It isn't necessary that students walk out of class with a fully articulated theology, but we hope to advance their thinking toward a more mature, more carefully thought-out set of beliefs.

To summarize, our goals in this course are:

1. To encourage students to ask serious, "tough" questions of being human, of religious belief, of meaning, and to share those questions with us.

2. To engage our students in conversation about these tough questions so that they understand that Judaism has a rich tradition of thought and reflection responding to these tough questions; to show our students that the Jewish tradition is itself an ongoing conversation about these tough questions.

3. To expose students to the multiple voices making up the historical Jewish conversation around these tough questions.

4. To guide students toward a more mature, more carefully thought-out set of personal beliefs.

A NOTE ABOUT THE TRANSLATIONS

Unless otherwise noted, the biblical translations are either mine or taken from the Jewish Publication Society's *Tanakh* (Philadelphia: Jewish Publication Society, 1985). The JPS translations do not use gender-neutral God language, and in an effort to preserve the authenticity of their translations, the author opted to leave them as they are.

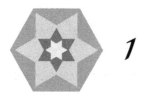

1

Am I Allowed to Ask?

GOAL

This lesson offers students the idea that questioning is an important part of Jewish religion and helps them begin to understand what it means to share a faith that is open to questions.

OPENING

Dear Rabbi,

I don't know what to do with my son. He's ten years old and just a bag of questions: If God is invisible, how do we know God's real? If God created everything, who created God? How do we know the Bible is true? When Grandma died, where did she go? Questions, questions, questions! It never stops!

When I was a girl, I learned that there were certain things you had to accept on faith. Questions weren't allowed! Especially about God. After all, who are we to ask questions about God? I was taught that beliefs had to be accepted and commandments obeyed, especially if they made no sense. That's the meaning of faith. And that's what God wants of us.

But my son…all he does is ask questions! Rabbi, I want you to explain to him that he must stop asking these questions and learn to accept our religion on faith, just like I did when I was young.

Thank you, Rabbi.

Yours,

Mrs. S.

ASK YOUR STUDENTS

If you were the Rabbi, how would you answer Mrs. S.'s letter?

If you were the Rabbi, what would you say to her son?

Do you agree with Mrs. S. that faith means accepting beliefs that make no sense to us?

Do you agree that's what God wants of us?

QUESTIONS FOR DISCUSSION

Do you have questions about God, about religion, about life that you've always wanted answered, but maybe were afraid to share them? Or maybe you couldn't find someone to answer them? Do you have questions you've always wished you could ask your rabbi?

Make a list of your questions.

There are religious people who believe, like Mrs. S., that we must accept beliefs and obey commandments even if they make no sense to us. What's the difference between a religion that demands acceptance and obedience and a religion that encourages questions?

Describe the ideal person shaped by each of these religions—a religion of obedience and a religion of questions.

> In the Torah, we're called *Yisrael*—the ones who wrestle with God. Wrestling, asking, wondering, searching is just what God wants us to do! God loves good questions! (p. 4)

Most religions, including Judaism, contain elements of both acceptance and questioning. Nevertheless, in the balance, Judaism strongly emphasizes questioning. What experiences of Jewish history do you think influenced this emphasis on questioning?

- Slavery in Egypt and the way we relive that experience each year at Passover?

- The experience of tyranny and anti-Semitism?

- The example of Abraham and other Jewish heroes who argued with God?

Are there dangers or disadvantages in encouraging people to ask questions and insisting that faith be built on understanding instead of obedience?

> Why are questions so important? Because we're Jewish with our entire self—our thoughts, our feelings, and our actions. We're not allowed to leave out any part of ourselves. The Torah teaches "You will love the Lord your God with all your heart, with all your life, and with all your strength" (Deuteronomy 6:5). Notice the word "all." Your whole self must be involved. You're not allowed to believe in something that makes no sense to you. You're not allowed to do things that feel wrong to you. Thinking, feeling, believing, and doing must be whole. (p. 5)

SOURCES

The ideal of the questioning Jew begins with Abraham.

> Then the Lord said, "The outrage of Sodom and Gomorrah is so great, and their sin so grave! I will go down to see whether they have acted altogether according to the outcry that has reached Me; if not, I will take note."
>
> The men went on from there to Sodom, while Abraham remained standing before the Lord. Abraham came forward and said, "Will You sweep away the innocent along with the guilty? What if there should be fifty innocent within the city; will You then wipe out the place and not forgive it for the sake of the innocent fifty who are in it? Far be it from You to do such a thing, to bring death upon the innocent as well as the guilty, so that innocent and guilty fare alike. Far be it from You! Shall not the Judge of all the earth deal justly?" And the Lord answered, "If I find within the city of Sodom fifty innocent ones, I will forgive the whole place for their sake." Abraham spoke up, saying, "Here I venture to speak to my Lord, I who am but dust and ashes: What if the fifty innocent should lack five? Will You destroy the whole city for want of the five?" And He answered, "I will not destroy if I find forty-five there." But he spoke to Him again, and said, "What if forty should be found there?" And He answered, "I will not do it, for the sake of the forty." And he said, "Let not my Lord be angry if I go on: What if thirty should be found there?" And He answered, "I will not do it if I find thirty there." And he said, "I venture again to speak to my Lord: What if twenty should be found there?" And He answered, "I will not destroy, for the sake of the twenty." And he said, "Let not my Lord be angry if I speak but this last time: What if ten should be found there?" And He answered, "I will not destroy, for the sake of the ten."
>
> When the Lord had finished speaking to Abraham, He departed; and Abraham returned to his place. (Genesis 18:20–33)

ASK YOUR STUDENTS

Why does Abraham think he has the right to challenge God?

Why does God allow him to do it?

What kind of religious ideal does this text celebrate?

What kind of faith and loyalty does Abraham demonstrate?

When is it okay to challenge those in authority? How should you do it?

TEACHER'S TIP: Abraham shares a covenant with God. *Covenant* means partnership. Partnership means that both sides must share common values and understandings. As God's partner, Abraham gains the right to question.

In contrast to this, the Torah presents a very different image of Abraham just a few chapters later. See Genesis chapter 22, the "Binding of Isaac," which presents a very different religious ideal. Faith and loyalty are expressed in silent obedience instead of protest.

ASK YOUR STUDENTS

How do each of these ideals find a place in Jewish life? In our lives?

When should we protest, ask questions, challenge?

When should we trust and obey?

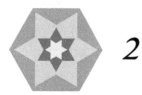

2

Who Believes in God Anymore?

GOAL

For the person who knows God, no proof is necessary. For the person who doesn't know God, no proof is sufficient. In other words, for the kid who insists that he or she doesn't believe, you'll never succeed in proving God's existence. What you can do is to show him or her that there are different ways of knowing. Very little of what we take for knowledge is actually "proven." Most knowledge is constructed, inferred, intuited, or sensed. By leading our students in this direction, we create an opening for knowing God.

OPENING

Read aloud the story on pp. 7–8 in *Tough Questions Jews Ask*: "A rabbi I know once asked a class of teenagers…"

ASK YOUR STUDENTS

Have you ever felt that God was close to you?

QUESTIONS FOR DISCUSSION

Believing in God is not a matter of accepting an abstract idea. Believing in God means gathering in the moments when God feels close and taking these moments seriously. It means remembering these moments, cherishing them, and saving them. It means pursuing them. And it means learning from them. (p. 9)

Consider each of the following:

- The Grand Canyon

- The wind

- Democracy

- Love

- Your best friend

How do you know about each of these? Each requires a different way of knowing. See if you can describe how you know each.

To know the Grand Canyon, you could visit and enjoy its beauty.

Wind is a physical phenomenon. You can feel it. But if you are indoors, you know it's windy outside by seeing what the wind does. You see leaves blowing about and you infer it's windy.

You can't see democracy only democracy in action—free debate, a free press, voting, government by the consent of the governed—and you intuit from this pattern of experiences that democracy exists.

How do you know about love? The only real way to know love is to experience it for yourself. You might put yourself in a situation in which you'd likely feel love then you would believe. Otherwise, you'd never understand.

To know a friend you might begin with other ways of knowing: Watch what he does, see him in action across many situations, intuit the patterns in his behavior. But to really say "I know him" you will have to do something else. You have to meet him, talk with him, do things with him. In meeting him, you come to know his qualities, the patterns of his behavior, what's special about him, and how it all adds up to a whole personality that is unique.

Which of these is most like God? These are all different ways of knowing. Which is the best way to know God?

> I believe that God is real. But God isn't far off in heaven; God is right here. How do we know God is near? By feeling the caring presence of others…. And by feeling our own power to care and to help. We can be God's hands, God's eyes, and God's ears in the world. We can bring God close to others when they are in need, just as others bring God close to us. (p. 12)

SOURCES

Rabbi Menachem Mendel of Kotzk was a great Hasidic master of the nineteenth century. Once, a student came and asked him, "Rebbe, where is God?" He answered, "Anywhere we let God in!" Here, another young man comes searching understanding and faith.

A young man once came to Menachem Mendel of Kotzk and complained, "Rebbe, I can no longer believe in God."

"Why is that?" the Rebbe inquired.

"I cannot believe in God because the world is so filled with pain, with suffering, with ugliness, and with evil. How could there be a God in such a world?" the young man answered.

"Why do you care?" asked the Rebbe.

"What do you mean, why do I care?" the young man asked, growing frustrated. "How could a person not care? Innocent people suffer, the world is ruled by the cruel and the heartless, its beauty is drowning in ugliness. I care because it hurts me so and I can't understand why a God would let it be this way!"

Again, the Rebbe inquired, "But why do you care?"

The young man grew more exasperated. "Someone has to care! Someone has to witness the pain of the world and cry. If not, then all the suffering is meaningless. If no one cries, then the universe is a dark, lifeless place. I care because I want with all my heart to see a better world for my children and for theirs. I owe it to them to care!"

And again, the Rebbe asked, "But why do you care?"

And now the young man lost his composure altogether and he wept. "I care. I have to care. I must. It's what and who I am."

"Well then," the Rebbe responded, "if you care that much, then God exists."

ASK YOUR STUDENTS

A young man complains that he's lost his faith in God. What's the Rebbe's answer?

How is caring evidence of God's existence?

If we don't care, does that mean God doesn't exist?

Why would the Rebbe choose the experience of caring as the single most powerful way of knowing God?

What else might be a way of knowing God?

3

What Good Is Praying?

I. Does God Listen? Does God Answer?

GOAL

Most people associate prayer with petition, asking God for something. This lesson introduces a different way of appreciating the purpose and value of prayer.

OPENING

A fable: Among those who left Egypt with Moses, there were two—Berel and Shmerel. As slaves, these two had grown so accustomed to looking down at the ground, they could no longer lift their eyes. And so when Moses brought Israel across the Red Sea, Berel asked Shmerel, "What do you see?"

"I see mud," Shmerel responded.

"I see mud, too. What's all this about freedom? We had mud in Egypt, we have mud here!"

When Israel stood at Mount Sinai, Shmerel asked Berel, "What do you hear?"

"I hear someone shouting commands," Berel answered.

"I hear commands, too. What's all this about Torah? They shouted commands in Egypt, they shout commands here!"

Finally after forty years, when Israel arrived at the Promised Land, Berel asked Shmerel, "How do you feel?"

"My feet hurt," Shmerel replied.

"My feet hurt, too. What's all this about a Promised Land? My feet hurt in Egypt, my feet hurt here!"

"As long as there's mud and shouting and hurting feet, we might as well go back to Egypt!"

And they turned around and went back. To this day, they're still slaves.

ASK YOUR STUDENTS

How many of the miracles of life do we miss because we're busy looking elsewhere?

QUESTIONS FOR DISCUSSION

> The purpose of prayer is not to change God. The purpose of prayer is to change us. The purpose of prayer is to make us aware of the miracles around us and the moments of God's closeness waiting for us each day. Prayer doesn't bring heaven down; prayer brings us up. So the question in the end is not, Does God hear my prayers? Rather, ask: Do I hear my prayers? Am I listening? Am I paying attention? Do I notice the miracles happening around me all the time? (pp. 16–17)

How does prayer change us? Change our way of looking at life?

What are the miracles happening to us all the time? How would we change if we noticed them?

SOURCES

Most Jewish prayer is not about asking for things. Most Jewish prayer is a way of becoming mindful—aware and appreciative—of the miracles happening to us all the time. The philosopher Abraham Joshua Heschel taught in his book *God in Search of Man* that this awareness is the most important part of religious life.

> Wonder, or radical amazement is the chief characteristic of the religious man's attitude toward history and nature. One attitude is alien to his spirit: taking things for granted, regarding events as a natural course of things. To find an approximate cause of a phenomenon is no answer to his ultimate wonder. He knows that there are laws that regulate the course of natural processes; he is aware of the regularity and pattern of things. However, such knowledge fails to mitigate his sense of perpetual surprise at the fact that there are facts at all. Looking at the world he would say, "This is the Lord's doing, it is marvelous in our sight" (Psalms 118:23).

To pray is to take notice of the wonder, to regain a sense of the mystery that animates all beings. Prayer is our humble answer to the inconceivable surprise of living. It is all we can offer in return for the mystery by which we live. It is gratefulness that makes the soul great.

We all know certain moments of life that are "Oh Wow!" moments. The religious person, according to Heschel, sees every moment of life as an "Oh Wow!" moment. Every moment is filled with miracle.

The opposite of religion, according to Heschel, isn't doubt or disbelief, but boredom—when we find nothing interesting or engaging in life. Prayer is a way of recovering the sense of "Oh Wow!" that belongs in every moment.

Every *bracha* is a reflection on the miraculous quality of everyday experiences. Even the most common experiences contain miracles. Here are three of the *brachot* said as we wake up in the morning.

Praised are You, Adonai our God, ruler of the universe, who opens the eyes of the blind.

Praised are You, Adonai our God, ruler of the universe, who clothes the naked.

Praised are You, Adonai our God, ruler of the universe, who frees the captive.

Ask Your Students

What miracles do they point to?

How would your life be changed if you noticed and cultivated the "Oh Wow!" moments in everyday life?

II. If I Pray for Something, Will I Get It?

Goal

This lesson suggests a distinction between magic and prayer. Magic is about changing the world. Prayer is about changing us. Magic removes our responsibility for the world. Prayer is about gaining the courage and ability to meet our responsibilities. Magic is pretend. Prayer is effective.

OPENING

Imagine the following appearing in a newspaper advice column:

Dear Jennie,

Every night this week, after putting my daughter to bed, I've listened in on her bedtime prayers. She prays to God to bring her a pony on her birthday. Her prayers are sincere and beautiful and truly from the heart. Jennie, there's no way we can afford to give her a pony. But when her birthday comes and there's no pony, she's going to conclude that God doesn't hear her prayers, or God doesn't answer her prayers, or that God isn't real. God is an important part of our lives and the thought of destroying her faith is killing me. What can I do?
Distressed

Dear Distressed,

Tell your daughter that God hears all of our prayers, and that God answers all our prayers. In this case, God's answer was, "No."
Jennie

ASK YOUR STUDENTS

What do you think of Jennie's answer?

How do you suppose the child will respond when she hears "God said, 'No'"?

What other answer could you give to this distressed parent?

Suppose the situation was different. Instead of a child praying for a pony for her birthday, suppose the child's parent had a deadly disease and the child was praying for her parent's recovery. Would you then also say "God said, 'No'"?

Does this answer really make it easier to believe in God?

How would you answer the person who asks you, in distress, "Why did God say 'No'?"

QUESTIONS FOR DISCUSSION

There is a difference between prayer and magic. A magician pretends to use his powers to change things in the world just by saying magic words. The most famous magic words are actually an old Hebrew spell: *Abra-Kadabra* is Hebrew for "I will make it as I say it."

We know that magic is not real. Rabbits don't come out of hats. And the lady isn't really cut in two and then reattached. It's pretend.

Expecting God to change the world just because you want it changed is also magic. And like magic, it's not real. It doesn't happen. God doesn't work that way. That's empty prayer. (p. 18)

What is the difference between magic and prayer?

If prayer doesn't change the world—it doesn't get you the good grade in school or the pony for your birthday—what does it do? What could it do for the person who is ill, or for that person's family?

SOURCES

The Talmud distinguishes between intelligent prayers and empty prayers. There are things we can ask God for and things we cannot. Here is the classic text distinguishing between the two:

> To cry over the past is to say an empty prayer. If a man's wife is pregnant and he says, "[God], let my wife have a boy!" this is empty prayer. If he is coming home from a journey and he hears cries of distress in the town and says, "[God], let it not be my house!" this is empty prayer *Mishna Brachot* 9:1. (*Brachot* 54a)

ASK YOUR STUDENTS

What makes these empty prayers?

What would make a prayer an intelligent prayer?

What can you expect prayer to accomplish? And what should you not expect of prayer?

4

Talking Snakes and Splitting Seas

I. Is Any of That Stuff in the Bible True?

GOAL

This lesson introduces the idea that the Torah can be morally true without being necessarily factually true.

OPENING

Read aloud the discussion of Thanksgiving on pp. 23–24 in *Tough Questions Jews Ask*: "On the fourth Thursday in November, people in the United States…"

ASK YOUR STUDENTS

> We all know this story, but is it true?
>
> What facts in the story are historically accurate? What's left out?
>
> Can the story be true even if all its facts aren't accurate?
>
> Why do we tell this story? What does the story tell us about being Americans?
>
> What does it mean to call oneself a "Pilgrim?" How is our American story a pilgrimage?

Questions for Discussion

Any schoolchild can find the problem in the story of Adam and Eve: If Adam and Eve had only sons (and one killed the other), how did the world get filled up with people? This inconsistency directs our attention away from the historicity of the story and toward its moral meaning. What truth is taught in the idea that all humanity is descended from the same mother and father? How does that change our perceptions of one another?

> The Bible tells us the most important truths about being alive. That's what makes it true. (p. 27)

Sources

When my daughter was in second grade, she came home from school one day very disturbed.

"Abba, we learned the story of Noah's Ark in school today and I wondered, when we went to the zoo, we saw so many animals. How did Noah get all those animals into one boat?"

Good question. So I told her a story that appears in the Midrash, the imaginative teachings of the third-century Rabbis:

> The Torah teaches that God saw that Noah was a righteous man. But the truth is, he didn't start out that way. What God saw was that he might grow into being a righteous man. That's why God chose Noah.
>
> Noah followed God's instructions. He built the ark, gathered all the animals, and on the day the rain started Noah brought them all on board and closed the doors. As soon as their journey began, Noah's son came running to his father. "Father, come quick! The lion is about to eat the sheep! Come quick!"
>
> So Noah ran down to the lion's place in the ark and sure enough, there was the lion ready to have the sheep for lunch.
>
> "Wait!" screamed Noah. "You can't do that!"
>
> "What do you mean I can't do that?" asked the puzzled lion. "It's lunchtime, I'm hungry, and I eat sheep for lunch almost every day!"
>
> "But not today," Noah tried to reason with the lion. "Today, you can't eat that sheep. You see, I only have two of them. And if you eat that one, there will be no more sheep on earth ever again."
>
> "But it's my nature to kill and eat. I'm a carnivore. That's who I am," responded the lion.
>
> "Yes, I know," answered Noah, "but for now, while we share this ark, you must put away that part of yourself. While we share this ark, you must protect the lives of all living things, not kill them."

"But what shall I eat?" asked the astonished lion.

"How about straw?" Noah proposed.

"Straw?!" The lion was truly appalled.

"Just until this is all over and we're off the ark. Eat straw," Noah instructed the lion. "In return, I will tell the world of your generosity and all the world will recognize in you qualities of strength they most admire."

"Very well," agreed the lion, feeling very regal. "Straw it will be."

Then another one of Noah's sons came. "Father, come quick, it's the elephants. They're playing and they're going to tip over the ark." So off Noah went to keep the elephants from tipping the ark.

"But we're playful creatures, it's our nature," complained the elephants when Noah asked them to stop. "How can we stop playing?"

"Just until we're home, stop playing and I will announce to the world how wise is the elephant."

"Very well, no more games," agreed the elephants.

So it was with the mosquitoes whose nature it was to bite and annoy others, and the pigs who messed everywhere and anywhere, and the monkeys who playfully stole others' food…. Each gave up a piece of its nature in order to share the ark on its journey.

ASK YOUR STUDENTS

And what part of his nature do you think Noah had to give up?

What truth does this midrash teach?

Is it true, even if the facts aren't accurate?

II. If God Talked to Everyone in the Bible, Why Doesn't God Talk to Anyone Today?

This lesson introduces the idea that there are many ways of hearing the voice of God, including hearing God's voice through the text of the Torah.

OPENING & SOURCES

The Rabbis of the Talmud offered a remarkable answer to this question.

> We have learned: A craftsman created a new design for an oven and brought it to the Rabbis to see if they would approve of his design. He cut the inside of the oven into separate tiles, placing sand between each tile. Rabbi Eliezer

declared it pure, but the Sages, the majority of the Rabbis, declared it impure.

On that day, Rabbi Eliezer brought forward every imaginable argument, but they [the other Rabbis] would not accept them. He said to them, "If the *halacha* [law] agrees with me, then let this carob tree prove it!" Thereupon, the carob tree jumped into the air a hundred cubits (150 feet). Some say it jumped four hundred cubits (600 feet).

"No proof can be brought from a carob tree," the Rabbis responded.

Again he said to them, "If the *halacha* agrees with me, then let the stream of water prove it!" Suddenly, the stream flowed backwards.

"No proof can be brought from a stream of water."

Again he said to them, "If the *halacha* agrees with me, let the walls of this academy prove it!" Suddenly the walls began to fall over onto the Rabbis.

But Rabbi Joshua scolded them [the walls], saying, "When scholars are engaged in a halachic dispute, what right have you to interfere?" So the walls did not fall in honor of Rabbi Joshua, nor did they stand upright out of respect for Rabbi Eliezer, and to this day they are still leaning over.

Finally, he said to them, "If the *halacha* agrees with me, let it be proved in heaven!" Then a Heavenly Voice was heard, "Why do you argue with Rabbi Eliezer—in *all* matters, the *halacha* agrees with him."

Rabbi Joshua arose and exclaimed, "It [Torah] is not in heaven."

Rabbi Joshua then quoted from the Torah, Deuteronomy 30:11–15. "This commandment I've given you today is not too difficult for you, not is it far away. It is not in heaven, that you should say, 'Who among us can go to the heavens and get it for us and give it to us that we may do it?' Neither is it beyond the sea, that you should say, 'Who among us can cross to the other side of the sea and get it for us and teach it to us that we may do it?' No, it is very close to you, in your mouth and in your heart, to do it."

What did Rabbi Joshua mean by this? His student Rabbi Yermiah said, "What Rabbi Joshua meant was that because the Torah has already been given at Mount Sinai we pay no attention to a Heavenly Voice, because You [God] wrote in the Torah at Mount Sinai, 'One must follow the majority' (Exodus 23:2)."

Rabbi Nathan once met Elijah the Prophet, God's special messenger, and asked him, "What did God do at that moment?"

"He laughed with joy," Elijah replied, "and said, 'My children have defeated Me, my children have defeated Me.'" (*Baba Metziah* 59a)

The year was about 120 c.e. The Rabbis argued over the status of a certain new design of an oven. Rabbi Eliezer, whose rulings usually found support among the majority of the Rabbis, on this occasion found himself alone, opposed by all the other Rabbis. To prove his point, Rabbi Eliezer brought all sort of arguments. But no one agreed with him. So he tried a different strategy, he brought a miracle. He made a tree rocket into the air. But the Rabbis were unmoved by his miracle. Rabbi Eliezer produced two more miracles, also unaccepted.

ASK YOUR STUDENTS

Why won't the Rabbis accept miracles as proof of Rabbi Eliezer's position?

What do the Rabbis lose if they accept miracles as proof?

TEACHER'S TIP: They lose the freedom to use reason to interpret the Torah.

Finally, Rabbi Eliezer produced the ultimate miracle. He brought God into the Academy and God said, "He's right!" That ought to prove it! There was no question that it was indeed God's voice. But the Rabbis rejected even that. Rabbi Joshua scolded God by quoting to God the words of the Torah, "It's not in heaven."

ASK YOUR STUDENTS

What does this mean?

Why won't the Rabbis accept God's direct instruction?

TEACHER'S TIP: They are turned into children, never able to decide for themselves, always waiting for God's instruction.

If they won't accept the direct word of God, how will we learn what God wants us to do?

How will we hear the voice of God?

TEACHER'S TIP: Using our own reason, imagination, and judgment to interpret the laws of the Torah.

The story has a remarkable ending. Rabbi Nathan was a mystic who had tea each Tuesday with Elijah, God's messenger. He begged Elijah to share with him how God responded at that moment. God, Elijah related, was overjoyed!

ASK YOUR STUDENTS

Why was God so happy?

When do parents celebrate being defeated by their children?

If God is the parent and we are the children, what does this story say about becoming religiously mature?

What must we do if we are to grow up spiritually?

God still speaks to us today. Not directly, but through the words of the Torah and the Prophets, the wisdom of the tradition, the symbols and rituals of our religion. When we think hard to understand the meaning of Torah and tradition, that's God's voice speaking through us. When we work hard making the dreams and ideals of the tradition part of our lives, that's God's voice showing us the way. When we teach others the wisdom of our tradition, that's God's voice teaching. Our sense of responsibility to God and to the Torah is an echo of the voice of God. (p. 30)

What's the difference between hearing God's voice directly and hearing God through the books of Torah and tradition?

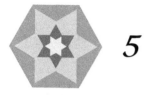

5

Why Does God Let Terrible Things Happen?

I. Why Does God Let Terrible Things Happen?

GOAL

This is the hardest question of religious belief, the most painful and the most personal. There is a conventional theology that assigns God responsibility for all the evil in the world, and then seeks to justify God's decisions. This lesson offers a different way to conceive of God and evil.

OPENING

Dear Rabbi,

Every year I've enjoyed coming to the synagogue for the High Holidays. I enjoy the spirit of the holidays, the music, seeing old friends, and feeling the warmth of the Temple. But this year, Rabbi, you won't see me and I want you to know why.

This year, as you know, my mom was diagnosed with breast cancer. She's had surgeries and painful treatment, and still we don't know what the future holds for her. You know my mom, Rabbi, and you know that there's no one nicer, kinder, more generous, and more committed to Judaism and to her family.

As the holidays got closer, I remembered that prayer we always say, the one that always gives me chills, "On Rosh Hashana it is written, on Yom Kippur it is sealed, who will live and who will die...." I realized then that this year I couldn't say these words. The prayer says that my mother's disease is God's decree, God's decision, and that God has reasons for this decree so that somehow my mother deserves what she's going through. This, I cannot believe. To sit in the Temple and hear you read these words would be too painful for me. So this year, Rabbi, you won't see me at the holidays. I'll be home with my mom.

Yours,

M.

ASK YOUR STUDENTS

How can we help M.?

QUESTIONS FOR DISCUSSION & SOURCES

The belief that God rewards and punishes is one way to understand the bad things that happen to us. This belief derives from the Torah. According to Deuteronomy, God is responsible for everything that happens to us. God rewards loyalty and punishes disloyalty. And God uses the forces of nature—rain, prosperity, fertility—as the tool of reward and punishment.

> If you obey the commandments that I command you this day, loving the Lord your God and serving Him with all your heart and soul, I will grant the rain for your land in season, the early rain and the late. You shall gather in your new grain and wine and oil. I will also provide grass in the fields for your cattle, and thus you shall eat you fill. Take care not to be lured away to serve other gods and bow to them. For the Lord's anger will flare up against you and He will shut up the skies so that there be no rain and the ground will not yield up its produce; and you will soon perish from the good land that the Lord is assigning to you. (Deuteronomy 11:13–21, which is read as the second paragraph of the *Shema* in traditional synagogues)

How might we respond to M.'s letter from the perspective of this belief in rewards and punishments? Is it comforting to believe that everything that happens to us comes from God? Does it help us to believe that God has a plan for the universe and even our suffering has a role in this plan?

Among the Rabbis of the Talmud, there were some who found this belief in God's rewards and punishments difficult to accept. They offer a different response to the problem of evil.

> Suppose a man stole a bag of seeds and planted them in his garden. What should happen? It would be right if the seeds didn't grow! But nature follows its own rules, and the seeds grow. Suppose a man had relations with his neighbor's wife. It would be right if she did not get pregnant. But nature follows its own rules, and she gets pregnant. (*Avoda Zara* 54b)

If Deuteronomy is right, stolen seeds and illicit sex shouldn't produce fruit, but they do. Because nature doesn't know right and wrong, nature has its own rules. We are bound to know suffering, not because God judged us, but because we are part of nature. How might we respond to M.'s letter from the perspective of this belief in nature's rules? Would she find it comforting? According to this belief, God isn't responsible for everything that happens to us. God may have a dream for the world, but God doesn't control what happens in the world. What, then, is the role of God in the world?

II. How Can Anyone Believe in God After the Holocaust?

GOAL

As in Lesson I of this chapter, this lesson offers a different way to conceive of God and evil.

OPENING

Read aloud the story on p. 35 in *Tough Questions Jews Ask*: "Recess was over and everybody came in to join the discussion…"

QUESTIONS FOR DISCUSSION

We have seen that there are two ideas in Jewish thinking of why people suffer. One idea teaches that everything that happens to us comes from God and God's plan for the world. The other teaches that God lets nature follow its own rules, even when that hurts good people, and therefore God isn't directly responsible for everything that happens to us.

The Holocaust is the single greatest act of human evil in the history of the world. How would each of these beliefs explain the suffering of the Holocaust? Is it better to believe that God has a plan for the world and this plan includes something as terrible as the Holocaust? Or is it better to believe that God leaves the world to follow its own course, even when that brings such terrible events as the Holocaust?

> God was not entirely absent from the Holocaust. God didn't check out…. God was present wherever human beings found the ability to resist the evil, to overcome the pain, to share kindness and care, and to get through the tragedy.

I'm sure you've heard of Hitler. You may even know the names of Himmler, Goering, Goebbels. These were the leaders of the Nazis. But have you ever heard of Joop Westerweel, Sempo Sugihara, Raul Wallenberg? Do you know who they are? (p. 36)

Everyone knows the story of Anne Frank. What were the names of the Dutch Christians who protected and provided for the Frank family? Everyone knows what happened to Anne Frank. What happened to those Christians? Were they ever recognized, thanked by anyone? TEACHER'S TIP: Raising this issue of Christian rescuers changes the way we teach the Holocaust. Beyond the endless Jewish suffering and the world's bottomless evil, we can begin a discussion of moral heroism and the righteous of all nations. Share the stories of Christian rescuers. If your class is able, watch and discuss *Schindler's List*. Locate a family in your community that was rescued and ask them to share their story. Share this unit with a local church class. Ask those who participate to discuss how these stories of Christian rescuers rescue their belief in God.

SOURCES

Emil Fackenheim is a German Jew, rabbi, professor of philosophy, and survivor of a Nazi concentration camp. After the Holocaust, he wrote in his book *God's Presence in History* (New York: HarperCollins, 1973) that Jews must learn important new mitzvot, new commandments, from these terrible events. Traditionally, Jews believe that the Torah contains 613 commandments. Now, taught Professor Fackenheim, we've been given the 614th commandment:

> Jews are forbidden to hand Hitler posthumous [*after death*] victories. They are commanded to survive as Jews, lest the Jewish people perish. They are commanded to remember the victims of Auschwitz lest their memory perish. They are forbidden to despair of man and his world, and to escape into either cynicism or otherworldliness, lest they cooperate in delivering the world over to the forces of Auschwitz. Finally, they are forbidden to despair of the God of Israel, lest Judaism perish.

ASK YOUR STUDENTS

Even though he's dead, Hitler can still win. How?

According to Professor Fackenheim, what is it that Jews are doing today that is giving Hitler the victory he never got when he was alive?

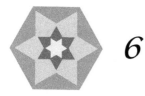

6

What Is God Anyway?

I. What Is God?

GOAL

Our goal in this lesson is not to teach a specific idea of God. Our goal is to give students permission to step beyond their childhood conceptions and "try on" some different beliefs. *Tough Questions Jews Ask* presents a number of suggestions on how we might think about God, from some very rationalist ideas to some very mystical ideas. Most important is that students recognize the variety of Jewish ideas of God and appreciate the implications of each idea. What difference does an idea make?

OPENING

Read aloud the dialogue between Josh and the Rabbi on pp. 41–42 in *Tough Questions Jews Ask*: "Josh knew sports. In the world of sports, he was a genius…"

We all have an idea of God in our heads. Even those of us who don't believe know what we don't believe in.

ASK YOUR STUDENTS

> What's your idea of God?
>
> Who is God?
>
> Where is God?

What is God?

How does God relate to the world? To you?

QUESTIONS FOR DISCUSSION

> Imagine the universe—the earth, the stars and planets, all of nature, everything that is, was, and ever will be—like a body. Is there a "self" living in this body? God is the "self" of the universe. (p. 43)

What difference does it make in the way we think about God, about ourselves, about the world, about other people, to say that the universe has a "self" and "God is the self of the universe?" How is this related to the *Shema Yisrael*?

> Imagine a wave on the ocean. Now imagine that God is the ocean and each of us is a wave. A wave is part of the ocean. A wave rises up out of the ocean to become distinct, and then it goes back again. Now, suppose the wave became aware of itself. It might think it was a separate, independent being. What would it take to make the wave discover that it was part of the ocean? And then how would it feel? How would that discovery change the wave's idea of itself? (p. 45)

TEACHER'S TIP: **The most powerful implication of this belief is the connectedness of all things and all people. We are all part of the One, the All. I cannot think of myself as a separate creature, independent of the environment I live in and the world I'm part of.**

II. What's That about God Being a Shepherd? Are We Supposed to be Sheep? Baaaaa!

GOAL

This lesson continues the discussion begun in Lesson I of this chapter that sought to encourage students to consider different beliefs about what God is. In this lesson, students explore the way the words and metaphors we use to describe God shape our beliefs. It encourages students to experiment with new kinds of "God-talk" in order to try out new beliefs about what God is and what role God plays in their lives.

Opening

Read aloud the continued dialogue between Josh and the Rabbi on p. 46 of *Tough Questions Jews Ask*: "OK, Rabbi," Josh continued..."

Questions for Discussion

> In the prayer book, we find lots of words describing God—Shepherd, Father, King, Rock, Healer, Redeemer. But these aren't meant to be literally true. God isn't really a shepherd herding sheep around. God isn't really a rock. These are metaphors. A metaphor, you will remember from English class, describes something by comparing it to something else. To unlock a metaphor, we need to find the common idea beneath the metaphor and what it refers to. (p.47)

Make a list of the most common metaphors for God. If you need help, open the prayer book. Now, go back and identify the quality each metaphor points to.

> God is a Shepherd. Just like a shepherd takes care of his sheep, we have a sense that God takes care of us. God is a Father. Just as parents love their kids, protect them, and provide for them, we have a sense that God loves us, protects us, and provides for us. God is King. Just like a king sets the rules of an empire, we believe that God gives us the rules for living a good life. (p. 47–48)

Having listed some of the tradition's metaphors, come up some of your own. We have a different vocabulary than our ancestors, what metaphors might grow from our experience? Make the same chart, listing the qualities that each metaphor suggests. For example:

- God is the universal Internet

- God is my phone system

Sources

The Jewish tradition has always been much more interested in what God does than what God is. Even in the Torah, God deflects Moses' question about God's essence with an answer about God's actions.

> He [Moses] said, "Oh, let me behold Your Presence!" And He [God] answered, "I will make all My goodness pass before you, and I will proclaim before you the name Lord, and the grace that I grant and the compassion that

I show. But," He said, "you cannot see My face, for man may not see Me and live." (Exodus 33:18–20)

TEACHER'S TIP: This emphasis on God's actions has led some thinkers to wonder whether it would be better to use the word "God" as a verb or adverb rather than as a noun. God is not a something, but a happening. Try this out on your students.

One last attempt to shake old beliefs: The common "default" idea of God is as a male, even though we all agree that God has no gender. Take any familiar text and translate it from masculine into feminine and listen to how it sounds. How does this change affect our thinking of God? What difference does it make in our religious lives to imagine God in the feminine?

> *The Lord is my shepherdess, I shall not want.*
>
> *She makes me lie down in green pastures,*
>
> *She leads me beside the still waters,*
>
> *She renews my life,*
>
> *She guides me on the paths of righteousness,*
>
> *For the sake of her glory.*

TEACHER'S TIP: Should you like to go further, some contemporaries have suggested that it's time we abandon all hierarchical metaphors for God such as King, Shepherd, etc., in favor of more intimate metaphors such as God as friend. Ask your students to experiment with writing new prayers in this mode.

7

What's the Meaning of Life?
Is That a Dumb Question?

GOAL

This lesson addresses this important question, perhaps the most important, and helps students understand that Jewish tradition has the resources to find an answer.

OPENING

Ask your students to make a list of famous people. Suggest reviewing a magazine like *People*, to see whom we celebrate.

Now ask students to separate their lists into two: Celebrities and Heroes.

ASK YOUR STUDENTS

What's the difference between a celebrity and a hero?

Do you have heroes of your own? Who are your heroes?

Who are your parents' heroes? Your teachers'? Your rabbi's?

QUESTIONS FOR DISCUSSION

The world we live in, according to an old Jewish tradition, is broken. Our world is filled with jagged edges and shattered pieces. We touch the world's broken-ness in all the evils we meet in the world—disease, violence, hate, war, hunger, poverty, and ignorance.

The world needs repair. God has invited us to share the work of repairing the world. That's what the Bible means when it says we have a "covenant" with God. We are God's partners. Our job is to repair the world.... There is a corner of the world that is yours. It is broken, and only you can fix it. It is a mess, and only you can make it beautiful. You were created with a special blend of abilities to do this job. You must find that corner and apply to it all your energies, talents, imagination, and intelligence. That's your mission. That's your purpose. And that's the meaning of your life. (pp. 53–54)

What's one thing you could be doing now, today, that would bring just a little bit of repair to the world?

SOURCES

The Haftarah portion (the prophetic text) for Yom Kippur from the prophet Isaiah 58:5–8 is a call for the responsibility God demands of us. The prophet begins by answering the people of his time who fasted and prayed piously on the holiday and expected God to respond with good times. But their fasting and praying was worthless, declared the prophet, because they failed to act as God's partners.

> Is such the fast I desire,
> A day for men to starve their bodies?
> Is it bowing the head like a bulrush
> And lying in sackcloth and ashes?
> Do you call that a fast,
> A day when the Lord is favorable?
> No, this is the fast I desire:
> To unlock fetters of wickedness,
> And untie the cords of the yoke
> To let the oppressed go free;
> To break off every yoke.
> It is to share your bread with the hungry,
> And to take the wretched poor into your home;
> When you see the naked, to clothe him,
> And not to ignore your own kin.
> Then shall your light burst through like the dawn
> And your healing spring up quickly.

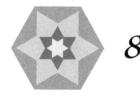

8

No Cheeseburgers?
No Going to the Mall on Saturday?
Why Does Religion Need so Many Rules?

GOAL

This lesson introduces a concept of mitzvot as religious rules designed to teach us to be better human beings.

OPENING

Who needs rules? Most of us have a sense that rules get in the way of our freedom. After all, who wants to be told what to do or what not to do? But sometimes, rules can help us grow into better people. By regulating our behavior, rules change the way we think and the patterns of our regular behavior.

ASK YOUR STUDENTS

How might each of the following kinds of rules make us into better people?

- The instructions of your piano teacher, your athletic coach, your ballet instructor

- Laws against using or possessing drugs

- Laws against discrimination on the basis of race, religion, or orientation in jobs, housing, and other opportunities

- School rules against hate speech or against ethnic or racial jokes

QUESTIONS FOR DISCUSSION

> If I'm going to help repair the world, I have to begin by repairing myself. I have to fix the broken parts of me—my violence, my hate, my greed, and my jealousy. I have to live differently, think differently, and look at the world differently. That's the purpose of these rules.
>
> The word for *rule* in Judaism is *mitzvah*. A mitzvah is, literally, God's commandment, God's rule. A mitzvah is God's tool in shaping human beings. A mitzvah teaches me to see the world through God's eyes. A mitzvah teaches me my power to work with God in repairing myself and repairing the world. A mitzvah is a way of teaching me to act Godly. (p. 65)

Sometimes, we divide mitzvot into two categories: ritual and ethical. But nearly all mitzvot have elements of both. They are ritual in that they involve symbolic behaviors. At the same time, they have the ultimate aim of changing and teaching us. The Jewish dietary laws are an ideal example. What's the big deal about a cheeseburger? How can it be so bad that Jewish tradition would prohibit it?

TEACHER'S TIP: Review the discussion of *kashrut* on pp. 59–61 of *Tough Questions Jews Ask*. Ask your students what they see is the purpose behind the laws of *kashrut*. What values do these laws reflect? Ask your students if they find this discussion compelling. Ask them, whether or not they observe *kashrut*, if these rules make sense to them.

SOURCES

A excellent example of the way mitzvot shape our attitudes and behaviors is the Jewish idea of charity. Unlike the conventional notion, charity in Judaism is not necessarily "from the heart." Rather, it is an obligation. Maimonides summarized the Talmud's teachings about charity in his famous "Eight Levels of Giving."

> MAIMONIDES, LAWS OF GIFTS TO THE POOR, CHAPTER 10
>
> We are obligated to be more careful in fulfilling the commandment of charity than any other mitzvah, because charity is the sign of the righteous person, the children of Abraham. There are eight levels of charity, one higher than the other.
>
> 1. One who gives grudgingly.
> 2. One who gives less than he should, but gives graciously.
> 3. One who gives only after the poor person has asked him.
> 4. One who gives personally before the poor person has asked him.
> 5. One who gives in a way that the recipient knows the identity of the giver, but the giver does not know the identity of recipient.

6. One who gives in a way that the giver knows the identity of the recipient, but the recipient does not know the identity of the giver.

7. One who gives in a way that is anonymous on both sides: the giver does not know the identity of the recipient, and the recipient does not know the identity of the giver.

8. One who assists a poor person by providing him a gift or a loan or by accepting him into a partnership or by helping him find employment—putting him into a position where he no longer needs other people's assistance.

ASK YOUR STUDENTS

Why is each successive level better than the previous level, but not as good as the one following?

What are the principles encoded in each of these steps?

Why must you give even if you don't feel like it?

Why is anonymous giving better?

Why is the last step the best?

How would following Maimonides' teaching change the way you think about poor people?

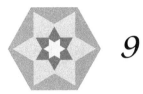

9

What Do You See When You Look at Me?

GOAL

Kids are obsessed with how they and others look. It's part of adolescence in our culture. This lesson introduces the idea that there might be other measures of individual beauty and worth besides looks.

OPENING

Here is a TV program I once saw: A teenage girl got so tired of the way boys "checked her out" and judged her—not on the basis of her personality, her talents, or her interests, but solely on her looks—that she devised an experiment. She filled up two balloons with warm water and stuffed them into her shirt. With her new "size," she went to a school dance. Suddenly all kinds of boys were interested in her. They wanted to dance and to chat. They offered to get her refreshments. They asked for dates. One young man was especially insistent. He found all sorts of clever ways to "accidentally" bump into her while they danced and talked. When she could stand it no longer, she reached into her top, extracted the two water balloons and handed them to him. "Here! If these are what you're so interested in, have them for yourself!"

ASK YOUR STUDENTS

> What's the problem with judging other human beings solely on their external looks?

> What part of us is left out of such judgments?

QUESTIONS FOR DISCUSSION

What would it take to look at a person and see not face or body or position but the infinite uniqueness and preciousness of that person? What would it take to learn to see every person that way?

The Bible's story of Creation includes the most remarkable idea about human beings: "God created man in His image, in the image of God He created him; male and female He created them" (Genesis 1:27).

> This is the strongest way the Torah could express the preciousness of each human being and the most powerful way it could demand that we value each person's uniqueness. The second of the Ten Commandments prohibits the making of images of God. So there is only one way to see an image of God in the world, in the character of each human being. When you see a human being, what you're to see is not just a face or a body, and not a pretty object, but a reflection of God. (p. 68)

What part of us is this "image of God"? If everyone carries God's image, how we perceive one another?

SOURCES

The Talmud powerfully expresses the importance of each individual human being.
> When God created the world, according to Genesis, God created flocks and herds of all the animals, but only one human being. Why did God create only one human being? To teach that one who destroys a single life, the Torah considers it as if he destroyed the entire world. And one who saves but a single life, the Torah considers it as if he saved an entire world.... This is an example of the greatness of God. For a human being mints coins with a single stamp, and they all come out looking the same. But God mints all human beings with the stamp of the first man, and yet each is unique. Therefore, every single human being must say, "For my sake, was the whole world created." (*Sanhedrin* 37a)

ASK YOUR STUDENTS

We begin by thinking of ourselves as unique and precious, then we learn to see others the same way. If we took this teaching very seriously, how would it change the way we treat one another?

 *10*

Why Are There So Many Different Religions? Aren't They All the Same?

I. Why Are There So Many Different Religions?

GOAL

Most people think of religious truth as a zero-sum game. For my religion to be right, yours must be wrong. This lesson introduces the idea that many different religions can be true simultaneously.

OPENING

Imagine the following scenario: Sometime in the future, people come to believe that the differences among the world's religions have been cause for conflict and strife among people long enough. To bring peace to the world, it is necessary to eliminate, once and for all, these differences. A United Nations commission is appointed to study the world's religions and take from each what is most valuable in order to create a World Religion of Peace that will be acceptable to everyone. The commission goes to work sifting through all the world's religions, taking the best of each. In the end, they produce a new Bible that contains this World Religion of Peace. Now there will be peace as everyone on earth will accept the same beliefs, celebrate the same holidays and rituals, and worship in the same way.

ASK YOUR STUDENTS

Is this possible?

Is it a good idea?

Would it bring peace?

Would you trade in your religion for this new World Religion of Peace?

QUESTIONS FOR DISCUSSION

Imagine a debate among proponents of the following beliefs:

- All religions have truth to teach. Religions should learn from one another.

- No religions have any truth to teach. All religions are false.

- Only one religion (or, only my religion) has truth to teach, all the others are false.

What arguments might each side present to prove its belief?

TEACHER'S TIP: If there is one God, why are there so many religions? Each of us feels that our religion is true and valuable. How can it be that different religions, teaching different beliefs, can all be true? And if they're all equally true, why not try a different one?

> Religions are like families. Each religion has its own stories, its own ways of celebrating special days, its own ways of talking to God. Each religion remembers the time when it felt closest to God.... By telling our religion's special story, we feel closer to the family of our religion and we feel closer to God.... Just as there is not just one right way to "do" dinner, there's no one right way to do religion. But that doesn't make dinner or religion interchangeable, any more than our families are interchangeable. (pp. 74–75)

SOURCES

The classic expression of Jewish universalism is connected to the moment of our greatest national triumph.

> And when Israel saw the wondrous power which the Lord had wielded against the Egyptians [at the Red Sea], the people feared the Lord; they had faith in the Lord and His servant Moses. Then Moses and the Israelites sang this song to the Lord. They said, "I will sing to the Lord for He has triumphed gloriously." (Exodus 14:31–15:1)

> At that moment, the angels of heaven began to sing praises to God. But God silenced them, saying, "My children are drowning in the sea and you want to sing before me?" (*Sanhedrin* 39b)

TEACHER'S TIP: On Earth, the Israelites celebrated their victory over Egypt. That's the Torah's story. The Talmud adds a second layer to this story. In heaven, the angels begin singing and are scolded.

For the same reason, we dip our wine during the recitation of the ten plagues—a silent midrash on that story, diminishing our joy because of the suffering of others.

II. What Is Christian Religion About? Is It Really That Different from Our Religion?

GOAL

For all the predominance of Christianity in America, it is remarkable how little Jewish kids know about Christian religion. It is not dangerous for Jewish kids to learn about Christianity. It is important to give Jewish kids permission to do so and this lesson will help. *Tough Questions Jews Ask* offers a brief account of the Christian story. You may choose to elaborate on the story, or bring in others who might help kids learn about our neighbor's religion.

OPENING

Read through pp. 77–83 in *Tough Questions Jews Ask* and ask students to keep a list of the core elements of each faith.

QUESTIONS FOR DISCUSSION

Review the list created in the opening exercise of this lesson. For Christianity, our list might include sin, the gap between God and human beings; Jesus Christ, God's son sent to earth to heal the gap; the Cross, the symbol of God's love; Jesus' Resurrection; Easter, the holiday that tells the story of Jesus' death and resurrection; salvation, escaping sin and earning afterlife.

For Judaism, our list might include covenant, the eternal partnership of human beings and God; Torah, God's wisdom shared with humans; mitzvot, the acts that bring God and humans close; *Teshuva*, the possibility of changing and reconnecting with God when we do something wrong; Yom Kippur, the holiest day of the year, a day dedicated to *Teshuva*.

What do Judaism and Christianity share? What are the principal differences?

TEACHER'S TIP: We share the Hebrew Bible, what Christians refer to as the Old Testament, and its faith in a loving God, its belief in the infinite preciousness of human beings, and in the call to live a moral life. We differ in our basic relationship to God, in our notion of sin and how we cleanse ourselves from sin, how we come close to God, and on the nature and importance of Jesus.

SOURCES

To get a sense of the similarities and differences between our traditions, let's examine an excerpt from an important Christian text, Matthew 5:21–22, 27–28, Jesus' Sermon on the Mount.

> You have heard it that it was said to the men of old: "You shall not kill," and who-ever kills shall be brought to judgment. But I say to you that every one who is angry with his brother deserves judgment; whoever insults his brother deserves judgment; whoever says "You fool!" deserves the hell of fire.... You have heard that it was said, "You shall not commit adultery." But I say to you that anyone who looks at a woman lustfully commits adultery with her in his heart.

ASK YOUR STUDENTS

> This is a midrash on the Ten Commandments. How does Jesus understand the commandments?
>
> What does he do with them?
>
> How is his understanding different from that of the Rabbis?

TEACHER'S TIP: Jesus begins with the Ten Commandments. But his understanding differs from the Rabbis. The Rabbis understood the laws against murder and adultery as laws against behaviors. For Jesus, they are rules governing attitudes. What are the strengths and weaknesses of each approach?

III. Can a Person Be Half Jewish, Half Christian?

GOAL

This lesson points out a fundamental difference between Judaism and Christianity.

OPENING

> Dear Rabbi,
>
> I'm Jewish and my husband is Christian. We are both involved in our religions. I go to the synagogue on Shabbat and my husband attends church most Sundays. We share the celebrations of each other's holidays. So far, our way of life has worked out.

We are about to have our first child and now we have a dilemma. You see, we would like to raise our child in both faiths, Christian and Jewish. We'll give the child the benefits of both. And so, it was our plan to have the child both baptized in my husband's church and blessed in the synagogue. When we discussed this with my husband's minister, he was dead set against it. He said it was impossible. He told us to go home, think deeply, pray, and make a decision to raise the child in one faith, not two. To say the least, we were devastated. Do you agree, Rabbi? Must we choose? Wouldn't our child be happier living in two great faiths rather than just one? And how could we ever choose? Would it make sense to let the child choose when he or she is old enough?

Yours,

J.

ASK YOUR STUDENTS

If you were the Rabbi, how would you answer J.'s letter?

Would you agree with the minister?

What help and advice would you offer this family?

Can a child be raised in two faiths?

What are the benefits and problems of such an approach?

QUESTIONS FOR DISCUSSION

Review the list of core beliefs from Lesson II of this chapter. A person who wished to be both Jewish and Christian would have to merge the two lists. Let's try. What items contradict one another? What items of one faith would the other faith find unacceptable?

The Christian idea of sin contradicts the Jewish idea of covenant. Jews can't accept the idea that Jesus was anything more than a man. Christians can't accept the idea of mitzvot, commandments God expects us to do. Jews believe they can always return to God in *Teshuva*. This is celebrated on Yom Kippur. Christians believe we can only return to God through Christ. Easter celebrates this. What other contradictions can we find?

> Christianity and Judaism often teach different things. Either you believe in Jesus or you believe in *Teshuva*. Either you celebrate Easter or you celebrate Yom Kippur.... Through the Cross, which symbolizes for Christians the life, teaching, death, and resurrection of Jesus, Christians come close to God.... The Torah is the Jews' symbol of God's love. Through the Torah, its commandments and teachings, Jews come close to God. Being a Christian is very admirable and beautiful. Being a Jew is equally admirable and beautiful. But being a "Jew for Jesus" combines things that are impossible to mix. (p. 81)

IV. Why Won't My Mom Let Us Have a Christmas Tree?

GOAL

This lesson helps students grasp the power of religious symbols, be they Jewish or those of other faiths. It guides students to understand some of the deeper implications of the presence of a Christmas tree in a Jewish home.

OPENING & QUESTIONS FOR DISCUSSION

A few years ago, there was a Paris fashion designer who took Jewish religious objects and used them for fashion accessories. *Vogue,* the world's most important fashion magazine, showed pictures of beautiful models wearing a tallit over a mini-skirt, tefillin as a kind of jewelry, and a *kippah* as a hat. How does that feel to Jews? How would we feel if a Christian family brought a Torah scroll into their home as a decoration, like a piece of art? (p. 83)

ASK YOUR STUDENTS

Is a Christmas tree a religious symbol, or just a pretty decoration for a special time of the year? Do you think that a religious Christian would agree with you?

What does it mean to bring the symbol of another religion into our home? What does it say to our Christian neighbors? What does it say about us? (p. 83)

11

Why Do People Hate Jews?

GOAL

The source of hatred for Jews is one of history's great debates. At least one option must be taken off the table: the ugly idea that Jews themselves are responsible. This lesson argues this point and turns the discussion into an examination of our own prejudices.

OPENING

In a very famous educational experiment, a teacher divided her class into two groups, brown-eyed kids and blue-eyed kids. She moved the brown-eyes to the front of the room and the blue-eyes to the back. She paid attention to the brown-eyes, complimented them on their conduct in the room, gave them privileges, all the while ignoring the blue-eyes. Whenever there was a problem in the room, she announced that the blue-eyes were at fault. At recess time, she put the brown-eyes in charge of the blue-eyes, giving them authority to enforce playground rules and the power to inflict punishments when there were infractions of the rules.

ASK YOUR STUDENTS

What do you supposed happened? How did each group behave?

What did this experiment prove?

QUESTIONS FOR DISCUSSION

Who is responsible for anti-Semitism? Many people hold the Jews themselves responsible, at least in part, for the hatred directed against them. Is this right?

What are the sources of hatred, prejudice, racism, discrimination, and stereotyping against any group, not just Jews? Why is prejudice directed at African Americans, Latino Americans, gays, and lesbians?

What's the role of fear, insecurity, and a sense of inferiority? What purposes does it serve those who hate?

> Jews have suffered for thousands of years not because anything they did was wrong, but because of the wrong thinking and evil behavior of those who persecuted them. Hate, anger, intolerance, small-mindedness, arrogance, evil—these are the reasons Jews have been made to suffer. (p. 87)

How does hate get started? Jews lived in Germany for seven hundred years prior to the rise of the Nazis. By the 1930s, they were thoroughly assimilated into German life—loyal Germans in every way and indistinguishable from anyone else in German life. So how did the Nazis persuade Germany to destroy them?

Trace the steps by which the Nazis destroyed the Jews of Germany:

- Identification—"There is a people living among us...."

- Castigation—"They are at fault for our troubled economy, our defeats...."

- Humiliation—"They are vermin infesting the Fatherland...."

- Isolation—Yellow Stars, ghettos

- Deportation

- Extermination

Are there groups in our own society whose treatment resembles what the Nazis did to the Jews? Can you see the beginnings of hate in your own school or neighborhood?

> We study it [the history of anti-Semitism] also to protect ourselves from becoming like the people who hurt us. We want to make sure we don't fall into the traps of evil, hatred, and prejudice against others that led to the destruction of so many of our own people. (p. 89)

SOURCES

In the Bible, we read of people who expressed a hatred of the Jews equal to that of the Nazis.

> A new king arose over Egypt who did not know Joseph. And he said to his people, "Look, the Israelite people are much too numerous for us. Let us deal shrewdly with them, so that they may not increase; otherwise in the

event of war they may join our enemies in fighting against us and rise from the ground." So they set taskmasters over them to oppress them with forced labor; and they built garrison cities for Pharaoh: Pithom and Raamses. But the more they were oppressed, the more they increased and spread out, so that the [Egyptians] came to dread the Israelites. (Exodus 1:8–12)

Haman then said to King Ahasuerus, "There is a certain people, scattered and dispersed among the other peoples in all the provinces of your realm, whose laws are different from those of any other people and who do not obey the king's laws; and it is not in Your Majesty's interest to tolerate them. If it please Your Majesty, let an edict be drawn for their destruction, and I will pay ten thousand talents of silver to the stewards for deposit in the royal treasury." (Esther 3:8–9)

ASK YOUR STUDENTS

Can you find the same steps in some familiar biblical stories of hatred and destruction?

12

If We Live Here,
Why Is Israel So Important?

GOAL

This lesson helps students understand the importance of Israel as their national homeland to Jews everywhere.

OPENING

Try the following as a guided visualization: Ever been away from home for a long time—on a long trip or at a summer camp? Remember what it's like to come home? You turn the corner onto your street and it feels special. It's not just any street. It's your street. Then you stop in front of your house and it feels even more special. Then you go into your room and you know you're home. All your stuff is there. Your memories of special times are there. It feels and smells like home. You know that you belong there.

TEACHER'S TIP: That's how the Jewish people feel about Israel.

QUESTIONS FOR DISCUSSION

The great Zionist leader and Israel's first prime minister David Ben Gurion argued that a Jew could only live a fully Jewish life in a Jewish country, in Israel. Was he right? We can certainly live a very full Jewish life in America. But what are some of the things we can't do as Jews unless we live in a Jewish country?

What special responsibilities go along with being a Jewish state? Do you think Israel must behave differently than other countries? Do you think it does?

SOURCES

There are many texts that reflect the love we share for the land of Israel and the city of Jerusalem.

> If I forget you, O Jerusalem,
>
> let my right hand wither;
>
> let my tongue stick to my palate
>
> if I cease to think of you,
>
> if I do not keep Jerusalem in memory
>
> even at my happiest hour. (Psalm 37:5–6)

13

Orthodox, Conservative, Reform? Why Can't I Just Be Jewish?

GOAL

This lesson offers the opportunity to discuss the character of each of the movements of contemporary Judaism. The best way to do this is to consider the strengths of each movement: What's best about Orthodox, Conservative, Reform, Reconstructionist Judaism? Try to avoid the triumphalism of contrasting the strengths of your movement and the weakness of the others. Our discussion will focus on the more general question of pluralism. How is it a virtue to have a faith with many expressions? How is pluralism possible?

OPENING

In the Torah's Book of Leviticus, we find a very famous commandment: "Love your neighbor as yourself." What does this mean? Make a list of all the possible meanings, interpretations, and applications of this commandment.

ASK YOUR STUDENTS

Who is your neighbor? Is he or she the person whose life is just like yours, or could your neighbor's life differ significantly from yours? Do your neighbors include only people who live close by, or those who live on the other side of the world?

What does it mean to love your neighbor? Is that a feeling or does it include behavior? What if you can't stand your neighbor—how do you love him or her? What if your neighbor is evil?

Why is the part about "as yourself" included? Why not just say "Love your neighbor"? What does the "as yourself" add?

Looking over your list of possible interpretations, which is the right one? Is it possible that there are numerous interpretations, all correct but all very different?

QUESTIONS FOR DISCUSSION

> There have always been different ways to be Jewish—different ways for Jewish people to experience God and to celebrate their being Jewish. (p. 98)

The Catholic religion has a pope, a central leader who decides the rules of the faith. The pope decides which beliefs, practices, and symbols are appropriate and which are inappropriate for the Catholic faith. We Jews do not have a pope. Why not? Would we be better off if we did? What problems would that solve? What problems would that bring?

What are the advantages and the disadvantages of having different forms of Judaism? Why are some people frustrated by the difference?

By considering our opening exercise, can you understand why we have differences? Judaism is a religion of interpretations. Interpretations will bring "pluralism," differences of opinion.

> Have you ever heard an orchestra playing a piece of music? As you listen, you realize that the musicians aren't playing the same thing. What makes orchestra music interesting is that each instrument, each musician, is playing something different. And yet, it all combines into one magnificent sound. Perhaps that's what God hears when we all practice Judaism in our different ways. To us, it sounds like conflicts and contradictions. But God hears the harmonies and the melodies and enjoys the music. (pp. 102–3)

Would the music be better if everyone played the same thing? On the other hand, if musicians in the orchestra were playing different pieces of music, instead of different part of the same piece, how would that sound? What are the limits of pluralism?

SOURCES

We are a religion of interpretation, which means we will always have serious differences of opinion. This requires a certain kind of temperament.

> For three years there was a dispute between the students of Shammai and the students of Hillel, one arguing, "The law is according to our view!" and

the other arguing, "The law is according to our view!" Then a voice from heaven proclaimed, "These and these are the words of the living God but the teachings of the School of Hillel will be the law."

It was asked, but if both are the words of the living God, why was the School of Hillel entitled to have the law according to its views?

Because they were kind and humble, and because they studied their own rulings as well as those of [their opponents], the School of Shammai, and even mentioned the teachings of the School of Shammai before their own teachings. (*Eruvin* 13a)

Rabbi Levi taught: God appeared to the Israelites at Mount Sinai as though He were a statue with faces on every side. A thousand people may look at the statue, but it would appear to each as though it were looking directly at him. So it is written, "I am the Lord your God" ["your" in the second person singular, not plural].

Rabbi Yosi bar Hanina taught: At Mount Sinai God spoke to each and every person according to his or her own particular ability. And do not wonder at this! For when the manna came down for Israel, each and every person tasted it in his or her own way—infants in their way, the young in their way, the old in their way…. David [author of the Book of Psalms] said, "The voice of the Lord is in its strength" (Psalms 29:4). Notice: the psalm does not say "in His strength" but "in its strength." That is, [the words were spoken] strongly enough to be heard and understood according to the ability of each and every person who listens to God's word. (*Peskita d'Rav Kahana* 12)

 *14*

What Happens to Us After We Die?

Goal

Many Jews think that belief in an afterlife is strictly a Christian preoccupation. In fact, Jews since the Bible have held strong beliefs in afterlife. In this lesson, we will show what is most important is the way our thoughts about death and our beliefs in afterlife shape our lives here and now.

Opening

Let's imagine for a moment a world in which no one died. People were born and lived forever. You had endless tomorrows. How would that affect the way people lived their lives and the choices people made?

Let's imagine a different world, where everyone knew exactly how long they had to live. Just as you know your birthday, you'd also know the day you would die. How would that change us? What advantages and disadvantages would such knowledge bring?

The Bible's Book of Psalms contains a remarkable statement: "Teach us to number our days that we may have a wise heart" (Psalms 90:12).

Ask Your Students

Why does the Psalmist want to number his days?

What wisdom is contained in that?

What wisdom can we learn from death?

QUESTIONS FOR DISCUSSION

> Life after death is not as important to Judaism as life before death. Life in the "next world" is not as important as life in this world. (p. 106)

Why does Judaism choose to think this way? What does it force us to accept? What's the problem with concentrating our attention on the "next world?"

> Our thinking about afterlife begins with a question about what it means to be human: Am I just a body? If I'm only a body, when my body dies, I die—I'm gone, and nothing lives on. Perhaps there is some part of us which is not body, not physical, so that when we die, this part goes on living. (p. 107)

How might a belief in afterlife affect our lives in the here and now?

SOURCES

In the sources that follow, notice how the belief in an afterlife is used to reshape our values in this life.

> "Open the gates of victory for me
> That I may enter and praise the Lord.
> This is the gateway to the Lord
> The victorious shall enter through it." (Psalms 118:19–20)

> When a person dies and goes up to the next world, he or she must stand before Judgment.
> They will ask: What was your occupation in the world below?
> If the person answers: "I fed the hungry,"
> They will say: "You who fed the hungry may enter [heaven]!"
> If the person answers: "I cared for the helpless,"
> They will answer: "You who cared for the helpless may enter!"
> And the same for the person who cared for abandoned children,
> And those who gave Tzedaka,
> And those who performed acts of love and kindness. (*Midrash Tehillim*)

TEACHER'S TIP: **Where is the question, what was your occupation? In that world, they are not interested if you were a doctor or lawyer or millionaire. In that world, other things are more important. When a person dies, we almost never remember what they had, only what they gave. In the face of death, there is a transposition of values. What is important then is not what is important now.**

Raba taught when a person is brought before Judgment [in the next world], they will ask:

Did you do business with honesty?

Did you find time for Torah learning?

Did you invest yourself in family?

Did you keep alive your hope for redemption? (*Shabbat* 31a)

ASK YOUR STUDENTS

Why these concerns?

How are these concerns tied to eternity and immortality?

15

What's the Messiah?

GOAL

As in the previous lesson, we want students to understand the importance of a belief in the Messiah lies in its effect on life in the here and now.

OPENING

If you could change one thing in the world that would make the world a better place, what would you change?

If you could change one thing about people that would make the world better, what would you change?

QUESTIONS FOR DISCUSSION & SOURCES

> Originally, the Messiah was to be the new king who would rule over the new, rebuilt Jerusalem. Soon the dream got bigger. The Israelites dreamed of a Messiah who wasn't just a king, but a messenger of God who would bring to life all their dreams—of a world of peace, love, and blessings. Some day, Jews told one another, the Messiah will come and make the world perfect. But when? (pp. 113–14)

Dreaming of a world made perfect is an old Jewish hobby. The question is, what would make for a perfect world? Here is the vision of the prophet Isaiah, who lived about 740 B.C.E. Describe the elements of his idea of a perfect world.

> In the days to come,
>
> The Mount of the Lord's House

Shall stand firm above the mountains

And tower above the hills;

And all the nations

Shall gaze on it with joy.

And the many peoples shall go and say:

"Come,

Let us go up to the Mount of the Lord,

To the House of the God of Jacob;

That He may instruct us in His ways,

And that we may walk in His paths."

For Torah [teaching] shall come forth from Zion,

The word of the Lord from Jerusalem.

Thus He will judge among the nations

And make peace for the many peoples,

And they shall beat their swords into plowshares

And their spears into pruning hooks:

Nation shall not take up

Sword against nation;

They shall never again know war. (Isaiah 2:2–4)

What is the opposite of this way of thinking? Perhaps a way that sees the world unchanging, never improving. In the Bible, that idea is reflected as well in the Book of Ecclesiastes 1:2, 9:

Utter futility!—said Koheleth—

Utter futility! All is futile!…

Only that shall happen

Which has happened,

Only that occur

Which has occurred;

There is nothing new

Beneath the sun!

Dreaming of a better world, even a perfect world, can give us hope and inspiration as we face the problems of our own world. But does this kind of dreaming have its own problems? Here are two Talmudic sources that try to keep a balance between our dreaming and the work we owe the world.

Rabbi Yohanan ben Zakkai taught: If you are planting a tree and someone comes along shouting, "The Messiah is here! The Messiah is here!" Finish planting the tree. Then go welcome the Messiah. (*Avot d'Rabbi Natan*)

Rabbi Tarfon taught:

The day is short, the task is great,

The workers are lazy, the reward is great,

And the Master is insistent.

You do not have to complete the work,

But never are you free to quit. (*Pirket* Avot 2:20–21)

16

What's a Bar Mitzvah?
What's a Bat Mitzvah?
Can't I Just Have a Birthday Party?

I. What's a Bar and Bat Mitzvah?

GOAL

Becoming Bar/Bat Mitzvah signals the arrival of adulthood. But what does it mean to be a Jewish adult? How is the Jewish idea of adulthood different from that in the general culture? Jewish adulthood is the focus of our discussion in this lesson.

OPENING

Imagine that you're a visitor from another galaxy who has come to observe and learn Earth culture. Watch an hour of television, any program you want, and make a list of the things that adults do and the qualities they represent. If you'd like, do the same exercise with movies, music, magazines, etc.

ASK YOUR STUDENTS

As a citizen of another galaxy, describe the adults you saw on TV. What are they like?

Now come home to earth. How are TV adults different from real life adults?

If people only learned about adulthood from TV, how might they grow up?

QUESTIONS FOR DISCUSSION

A birthday party is about becoming another year older. A Bat or Bar Mitzvah is about becoming an adult. What does that mean, becoming an adult? What does American culture teach us about being an adult? What does Jewish tradition say about it?

> In Jewish life, becoming an adult…means being responsible. It means that your family, your community, and God can count on you. We count on you to do your part in helping us to fix all the broken parts of the world—hunger, disease, hurt, war. We count on you to help bring the world close to God's dream. That's hard work. But it feels special knowing that people count on you. It feels special knowing that you're important enough that people expect something from you. (p. 117)

What does it mean to become an adult? What privileges come with adulthood? What responsibilities? What are you looking forward to most? What are you most afraid of?

SOURCES

Pirke Avot, the Wisdom of the Sages, is a Talmudic book that contains no law, only wise sayings by the great Rabbis. It is a book all about becoming a Jewish adult. Here are two important selections.

> Hillel used to say: If I am not for myself, who is for me?
> but if I am only for my own self, what am I?
> and if not now, when?
> (*Pirke Avot* 1:14)

ASK YOUR STUDENTS

> What does Hillel mean?
>
> Are the first two lines contradictory?

> Rabbi Shimon Ben Zoma said, who is wise? One who learns from all people, as it is said: "From all who taught me have I gained understanding" (Psalms 119:99).
>
> Who is strong? One who conquers his/her own drives, as it is said: "He that is slow to anger is better than the mighty; and he that rules over his own spirit than he that conquers a city" (Proverbs 16:32).
>
> Who is rich? One who is happy with what s/he has, as it is said, "When you eat the labor of your hands, happy will you be and all will be well with you" (Psalms 128:2).

Who is respected? One who honors all people, as it is said: "Those who honor Me will I honor..." (I Samuel 2:30).

TEACHER'S TIP: To understand Ben Zoma's wisdom, ask yourself, what common opinions is he arguing *against*?

Who is wise? One who has degrees from Harvard? For Ben Zoma, every person has something to teach. But what qualities of character does it take to learn from everyone?

Who is strong? Arnold Schwarzenegger? Perhaps the head of a state who controls armies? But what controls him? If he cannot control himself, what good is his power? Notice that Ben Zoma does not teach, "one who destroys his impulses." Impulses—hunger, desire, greed, envy—make us human, as long as we can control them.

Who is rich? The one who has much but is ruled by greed for more or the person who has less but is satisfied with what she or he has?

Who is honored? The one with awards, medals, and plaques? Or the esteem of those who enjoy her or his presence?

11. Why Do We Have to Keep Going to Hebrew School Even After We're Bar Mitzvah?"

GOAL

This lesson guides students to understand that continuing Jewish education past Bar/Bat Mitzvah is important to life as a Jewish adult.

OPENING & QUESTIONS FOR DISCUSSION

> Why do you go to regular school? Why bother with high school, let alone college? You're a teen now—a young adult. You've probably been in school since you were two or three years old. You know how to read and do basic math. You know a few dates in American history. What else do you need to know? What can they teach that you don't already know? (p. 119)

Why do we go to school? Most people would say to learn, to get good grades and get into college, to get a good job, and to earn enough money to live a good life.

Are there any other reasons? How about learning and growing as a person; becoming an educated person; the fascination of ideas, knowledge, literature; the experience of discovery.

But if these are the reasons, then there really is no such thing as finishing one's education.

> The answer, of course, is that there is a whole world of knowledge and wisdom that your early years in school have only prepared you to discover. The best is yet to come. (p. 119)

In America, we learn in order to make a living. In Judaism, it's the other way around. One makes a living in order to have time to learn. Learning is a life-long adventure.

> Jewish culture is the collective wisdom of our civilization, passed to you in literature, symbols, and custom. We call this conversation Torah. Study Torah and you are invited to join one of the world's longest and deepest ongoing conversations about being human.... Hebrew school has only given to you the beginnings, the basic tools. Now, you're almost ready to join the great conversation. And once you do, you're never finished. In Jewish life, you never finish learning—there's no such thing as "graduation." (p. 120)

SOURCES

Our masters taught: Once the wicked Roman government issued a decree forbidding the Jews to study and practice the Torah. Pappus ben Judah came by and, finding Rabbi Akiba publicly holding sessions in which he taught Torah, asked him, "Akiba, are you not afraid of the government?"

Rabbi Akiba replied, "You, Pappus, who are said to be wise, are, in fact, a fool. I can explain what I am doing by means of a parable: A fox was walking on a river bank and, seeing fishes hastening here and there, asked them, 'From whom are you fleeing?' They replied, 'From the nets and traps set for us by men.' So the fox said to them, 'How would you like to come up on dry land, so that you and I may live together the way my ancestors lived with yours?' They replied, 'You—the one they call the cleverest of animals—are, in fact, a fool. If we are fearful in the place where we can stay alive, how much more fearful should we be in a place where we are sure to die!' So it is with us. If we are fearful when we sit and study the Torah, of which it is written, 'For this [Torah] is your life and the length of your days' (Deuteronomy 30:20), how much more fearful ought we to be should we cease the study of Torah?"

Soon afterward, Rabbi Akiba was arrested and thrown into prison, and Pappus ben Judah was also arrested and put into prison next to him. Rabbi Akiba asked, "Pappus, what brought you here?"

He replied, "Happy are you, Rabbi Akiba, that you have been seized for occupying yourself with Torah! Alas for Pappus, who has been seized for occupying himself with worthless things!"

When Rabbi Akiba was to be taken out and executed, it was the hour for reciting the *Shema*. The executioners were combing his flesh with iron combs, while he was lovingly making himself ready to accept upon himself the yoke of the kingship of heaven (i.e., to recite the *Shema*).

His disciples asked, "Our teacher, even now?"

He replied, "All my days I have been troubled by this verse, 'Love the Lord your God...with all you soul' (Deuteronomy 6:5) which I have interpreted as meaning, 'Even if He takes your soul.' But I said, 'When shall I have occasion to fulfill the precept? Now that I have the occasion, shall I not fulfill it?"

He prolonged the *Shema's* concluding word, *ehad*—One—until he expired. A divine voice went forth and proclaimed, "Happy are you, Akiba, that your soul has departed with the word *ehad*! (*Brachot* 61b)

ASK YOUR STUDENTS

Why did Rabbi Akiba risk torture and death to teach Torah?

 *17*

Why Is It So Important to Marry Someone Jewish?

I. Why Is It Important to Marry Someone Jewish?

GOAL

This lesson makes the case for in-marriage by demonstrating the difference between falling in love and loving over the long-term. For kids raised on American images of romance, this can challenge some deeply held beliefs.

OPENING & QUESTIONS FOR DISCUSSION

Remember the movie *The Little Mermaid*? This was a charming children's story about a beautiful mermaid who wanted to marry a handsome human prince. She was in love with him!

It turns out that the story has two different endings: In the Disney film, she gets the guy, and her father, the King of the Sea, comes to the surface to bless their marriage. In the original Hans Christian Anderson story, she fails to get the prince's love and she disappears into the mist.

What's behind these two endings? In the world of Disney, it matters little how different you are as long as you're in love. Does that really work? For how long? What does it mean to love someone? What's the difference between falling in love and being in love for life?

In Hans Christian Anderson's story, there's more to love than a momentary feeling of desire. Long-term love requires something else. What else is needed to share life together?

Here's a hint. I took my then nine-year-old to see the film. He loved it. But on the way out of the theater, he asked me, "Dad, what do you suppose happens next? Like the week after they're married and he wants a tuna sandwich and she discovers he's eaten her Uncle Charlie? Could they really live happily ever after? What do you think?"

ASK YOUR STUDENTS

> In the long term, do you think the Little Mermaid will be happy living with the prince?
>
> Do these relationships work?
>
> What would it require for this to work out?

> People can fall in love with others who are very different. We can have intense relationships with others whose values and interests and ideas and backgrounds are very different. But these relationships rarely last long. Eventually, we get tired of all the compromising that such relationships require. We get tired of giving up the things that mean so much to us....Then, we go looking for someone whose values and interests and ideas are more like our own. (p. 124)

II. What If I Fall in Love with a Person Who Isn't Jewish but Wants to Be? Can Someone Join Up?

GOAL

This lesson introduces students to the concept of conversion to Judaism and invites them to consider the joys and complications converting can bring.

OPENING

Make a list of ten things you think a person would have to know to become Jewish.

ASK YOUR STUDENTS

> Why would someone born into another faith want to become Jewish?
>
> What do you suppose is the hardest thing for a person becoming Jewish to get used to in Jewish life?

QUESTIONS FOR DISCUSSION

> Since the time of Abraham and Sarah, the Jewish people have welcomed outsiders who wish to join us.... Once a person has completed the learning process and these rituals, we give the person a Hebrew name and the designation *ben-* or *bat-Avraham v'Sarah*—children of Abraham and Sarah. These people are never called "converts." They are fully and completely Jewish and welcomed warmly into the Jewish community. (pp. 127–128)

Why are those who join us never called "converts"? Why do we give them such an honorary title as *ben-* or *bat-Avraham v'Sarah*?

Despite the fact that Jewish tradition warmly accepts and celebrates those who enter our faith from outside, there are many Jews who simply won't accept them. Why do you suppose that is? What motivates this rejection? How do you suppose it feels to the newly Jewish person to be rejected by others Jews?

SOURCES

In the sources that follow, we can sense the tension between those who sought to enter the Jewish faith and those who would exclude them.

> In the Bible, there is a story of a woman named Ruth. She marries a Jewish man who soon dies. When her husband's mother tells her to go home, go back to her people, she answers with great power and beauty, "Don't tell me to leave you, to turn away and not follow you. Wherever you go, I will go. Where you live, I will live. Your people will be my people and your God will be my God. Where you die, I will be buried. And nothing but death will separate me from you" (Ruth 1:16–17).

Ruth remarried a member of her husband's family and had children. The Bible tells us that Ruth was the great-grandmother of King David, the greatest king of Israel, who is himself the ancestor of the Messiah. Recall that the Messiah represents the ultimate fixing of the world. The Book of Ruth teaches that we start the process of fixing the world when we welcome the outsider who wishes to become part of us.

> A convert named Ovadia was barred from praying with the congregation because some questioned how he could offer prayers to the "God of our ancestors." Ovadia wrote to the great sage Maimonides with this question: Is a convert a real Jew? With all his power Maimonides responded, "Anyone who becomes a convert is a pupil of our father Abraham and all of them are

members of his household. You may say, 'God of our ancestors' for Abraham is your father...and there is no difference between us and you.

"Toward father and mother we are commanded to show honor and reverence, toward prophets to obey them, but toward converts we are commanded to have great love in our hearts...God in His glory loves the convert."

18

Why Be Jewish?

GOAL

This lesson culminates and summarizes all our other lessons. In it, we reiterate the idea of being God's partner as the central idea of being Jewish.

OPENING

Dear Rabbi,

You remember my son—you were at his Bar Mitzvah! Now he's in college and just yesterday I received a letter from him telling me that he wants nothing to do with being Jewish anymore. It's not that he's adopted another religion. He rejects all religions but especially Judaism. Judaism, he says, has no point and nothing to say to him, nothing to contribute to his life.

Rabbi, I've always felt very Jewish. This letter breaks my heart. What can I say to my son that might bring him back to being Jewish? Would you talk to him?

Yours,

Mrs. H.

ASK YOUR STUDENTS

How would you answer Mrs. H.'s note?

Is there anything she could say to her son?

Is there anything the Rabbi could say?

Is there anything Mrs. H. might have done before her son went off to college to prevent this situation?

QUESTIONS FOR DISCUSSION

> The biggest, most important job you have right now is writing the story of your life. You are its author, its illustrator, its publisher. You decide its plot, its themes, its lesson. You get to decide what's going to happen next…. If you don't make the choice to shape your life carefully and with wisdom, there are forces all around that will do it for you. If you don't live life on purpose, you'll live by accident. (p. 130)

What does it mean to "live by accident"? If you were going to write the story of your life, what kind of story would it be?

Many people start out believing that they are Jewish just because they were born Jewish or because they grew up in a Jewish home. It's just what they are. Perhaps that applies to just "being Jewish." But living Jewishly involves making a choice—in fact, many choices. Why should you make such a choice? What difference does it make in your life?

> Here's my hope for you: Be a hero.
>
> A hero need not be famous. A hero isn't just the firefighter who rushes into the burning building to save someone's cat. A hero is someone who has made his or her life into a symbol of something higher and greater. A hero is a person whose life matters…. Judaism teaches us how to live the life of a hero. (pp. 130–131)

What are the ways Judaism prepares us to live the life of a hero?

SOURCES

The most exciting moment in the entire Torah has to be the story of the Splitting of the Red Sea. Everyone remembers the story.

> The Splitting of the Sea is the most exciting moment in the entire Torah. The Israelites, having escaped from Pharoah's slavery, hastily ran from Egyptian bondage into the desert. As they camped on the banks of the Red Sea, Pharoah's heart was hardened one last time and he resolved to pursue the Israelites and to slaughter them. His chariots came charging across the desert.
>
> The Israelites found themselves trapped, with the impassable Sea on one side and charging armies of Pharoah's chariots on the other. They cried bitterly to Moses, who raised his eyes to God in prayer. God admonished him, this is not the time for prayer. "Command the Israelites to move forward. Hold your staff over the Sea, and it will split, and you will cross in safety."

This Moses did and his people crossed in safety. When Pharoah's troops followed them, the Sea returned and drowned them all.

But the Rabbis of the Midrash read the story differently.

Moses prayed to God. He held his staff over the Sea, but the Sea didn't split. He tried again, but the Sea did not move. Then he became nervous, frantic. He tried to recall the exact words of God, the exact instructions. Again, he held the staff over the waters but they did not move. He panicked. The people panicked. Everyone was frenzied with fear. And no one knew what to do.

No one except Nachshon ben Aminadav, a prince of the tribe of Judah. Nachshon understood that God was waiting. God had sent Moses. And God had brought the plagues. And God had led them out of Egypt. Now God was waiting for the people to take some role in their own rescue and liberation. God would not split the Sea until someone moved, until someone was ready to risk their own life to earn freedom. And so Nachshon jumped in. At first, everyone looked at him with wonder and awe. "What are you doing?" his family shouted. But he paid no heed. He knew exactly what he was doing. As he waded out farther, the water covered his knees. His family screamed and shouted, but he went farther, until the water covered his waist. Then, everyone stood silently watching. He waded farther, until the water covered his shoulders. And then a few more steps until the water covered his nostrils. He could no longer breathe. Then, only then, did the Sea split and Israel crossed in safety. (*Mechilta Beshalach*)

ASK YOUR STUDENTS

The world isn't rescued unless we jump in. But what does it take to have the courage to jump in?

About Jewish Lights

People of all faiths and backgrounds yearn for books that attract, engage, educate, and spiritually inspire.

Our principal goal is to stimulate thought and help all people learn about who the Jewish People are, where they come from, and what the future can be made to hold. While people of our diverse Jewish heritage are the primary audience, our books speak to people in the Christian world as well and will broaden their understanding of Judaism and the roots of their own faith.

We bring to you authors who are at the forefront of spiritual thought and experience. While each has something different to say, they all say it in a voice that you can hear.

Our books are designed to welcome you and then to engage, stimulate, and inspire. We judge our success not only by whether or not our books are beautiful and commercially successful, but by whether or not they make a difference in your life. They cover all the categories of your life:

Bar/Bat Mitzvah	Grief / Healing	Prayer
Bible Study / Midrash	Holidays / Holy Days	Ritual / Sacred Practice
Children's Books	Inspiration	Spirituality
Congregation Resources	Kabbalah / Mysticism / Enneagram	Theology / Philosophy
Current Events / History	Life Cycle	Travel
Ecology	Meditation	Twelve Steps
Fiction: Mystery, Science Fiction	Parenting	Women's Interest

The Book of Miracles   AWARD WINNER!
A Young Person's Guide to Jewish Spiritual Awareness
by Lawrence Kushner
Introduces kids to a way of everyday spiritual thinking to last a lifetime. Kushner, whose award-winning books have brought spirituality to life for countless adults, now shows young people how to use Judaism as a foundation on which to build their lives.
6 x 9, 96 pp, HC, 2-color illus., ISBN 1-879045-78-8

For Kids—Putting God on Your Guest List
How to Claim the Spiritual Meaning of Your Bar or Bat Mitzvah
by Rabbi Jeffrey K. Salkin

For ages 11–12

An important resource for kids ages 11 and 12, to help them spiritually prepare for their bar/bat mitzvah.

Salkin instructs, engages and inspires in a language young people can understand to teach the core spiritual values of Judaism. Discussion questions at the end of each chapter give them the opportunity to engage with the text, process what they have learned, and offer their own thoughts.
6 x 9, 144 pp, Quality Paperback ISBN 1-58023-015-6

The Story of the Jews
A 4,000-Year Adventure—A Graphic History Book
Written and illustrated by *Stan Mack*
Through witty cartoons and accurate narrative, illustrates the major characters and events that have shaped the Jewish people and culture. For all ages.
6 x 9, 304 pp, Quality PB, Illus., ISBN 1-58023-155-1

Printed in the USA
CPSIA information can be obtained
at www.ICGtesting.com
LVHW081029080824
787694LV00005B/492